TALES FROM NIGERIA-IBIBIO:

Some Legends and Myths

OTHER BOOKS BY THIS AUTHOR:

African Culture Through Proverbs;

Culture of Names in Africa: A Search for Cultural Identity;

Nigerian-Ibibio Riddles Idioms and More Proverbs;

Mmama Tells Stories: How Tortoise Got its Shell Cracked, Vol. 1;

Mmama Tells Stories: How Tortoise Got its Shell Cracked, Vol. 2;

The Wisest King Who Died at a Fool's Door-Steps and Other Stories.

TALES FROM NIGERIA-IBIBIO:

Some Legends and Myths

Emma Umana Clasberry

Tales from Nigeria-Ibibio: Some Legends and Myths.

ISBN-13: 978 - 1500227562

ISBN-10: 1500227560

First printed in the United States of America.

Font size and style: 13 and Century Schoolbook.

Create Space, Inc.

DEDICATION

To those who have written down these stories.

TABLE OF CONTENTS

INTRODUCTION

In earlier times, in the late 14th century, the word, legends, referred to stories that were written about the lives of saints. But later, from around the 15th century till present, the word has been used to describe written stories and those transmitted by words of mouth from generation to generation.

Legends popularly describe events that are believed to have actually taken place in history about a particular and real people, at a particular and real locality, and at a particular historical period. It does not matter whether the stories are entirely believable or not, partially true or not, or entirely verifiable or not. They do in fact reflect a people's collective experiences and beliefs, and shape their commonly held values. Legends often leave relics as bases of

7

truth and relevance to the people's daily activities.

Legends are similar to myths in the sense that actors in both of them may involve super -natural beings like gods and semi-gods, and natural beings, including humans. Myths attempt to explain natural and super-natural phenomena in general. An example of a myth is the story about why the Sun now lives in the sky.

But a legend explains a particular event, regarded as historical, although it may not be verifiable, that has shaped the beliefs and traditional practices of a particular people at a particular place. The *Idio* land holding concept, for example, practiced today in some parts of Ibibio originated from the story about how the Almighty God came down in the form of a whirlwind to help humans in farm work.

Out of the six stories presented in this work, the first three are legends and the last three are myths. Actually, there is a fine line between legends and myths in terms of actors, and they can exchange platforms easily. However, legends and myths, like tall tales and fables, are folk tales -stories passed down by ordinary people by words of mouth from generation to generation, and their authors are not known.

Unlike fables and tall tales that aim at teaching morals, social values and skills, and at enhancing common sense, legends and myths are usually retold to explain why some natural and super-natural phenomena are the way they are today.

Legends and myths are not generally retold in children's story telling sessions as we retell fables, partly because they are mainly for knowing or information purposes. Instead, they are mainly learned through listening to daily casual conversations by our elders or other knowledgeable persons. Also, it is a common practice for parents, mostly mothers, to retell these tales to their children in a casual way, and not necessarily in a typical story telling setting. We can learn by reading relevant books in school or through self-directed readings or field studies as well.

However, we should not be surprised to see some myths or legends sometimes showing up during story telling sessions that usually focus on retelling fables, especially if they have desirable moral lessons, and other valuable social values and skills to offer to the readers or listeners.

HOW WOMEN LOST THEIR RULING POWER

Long ago, women were always part of the ruling class in Ibibio traditional culture. In the days when inter-tribal wars were common occurrences, unmarried adult daughters had the obligation to defend their family or village lineage directly and indirectly. They had to protect and preserve their father's rights to the disputed lands by acting as secret agents. They reported on all war enemies and their activities to their father's lineage. This duty was particularly required of them during wars resulting from disputes between clans or between villages over rights to lands.

Upon marriage, the daughters were still expected to continue to perform the duty of defending their father's village or clan lineage by working as secret agents during tribal wars resulting from land disputes. They eavesdropped on the enemy and reported to their father's clan or tribe. Even where a war was between their husband's village or clan and their father's lineage, they were still mandated by tradition to spy on their marital family and report against their marital family in favor of their father's family.

The duty of a secret agent was required of married daughters by their fathers because their fathers did not see them as being part of or belonging to their marital families. They were not even required to change their names to husbands' surnames when they married because their fathers' traditions did not allow them to fully claim or identify with their husband's lineage.They remained unshakably part and parcel of their father's lineage. For this reason, they had to continue serving as undercover agents and indirectly defending the rights of their fathers to their lands even up to when they were in their marital homes.

Also, married daughters had to defend

their fathers' lands partly because the lands belonging to their husband's family were not theirs; instead, they were their sons'. The people's tradition did not grant, let alone guarantee, daughters any inheritance of their father's estate either. But it did grant and guarantee all daughters, unmarried and married, the rights to a *"six feet land"* inheritance, a burial ground.

Through the *six-feet land* injunction as compensation to married daughters for their active role as secret agents in times of inter-tribal wars over rights to disputed lands, their fathers' lands indirectly belonged to them. They were therefore obliged to work together with their fathers' family lineage in the face of external threat to defend their rights over the lands under dispute. In other words, the people's custom mandated all married daughters to join with unmarried daughters in protecting and preserving their fathers' rights to the ownership of the disputed lands.

There was another reason why the six-feet

land space was given and guaranteed to all married daughters. Fathers expected their married daughters to be returned at death to their paternal family and be buried near their ancestors so as to continue to live as a family and serve their ancestors as secret agents in the world yonder, as they did on Earth.

The burial land space inheritance was not the only compensation to daughters for their active involvement as spies in defending their fathers' lands. In those days, chiefs were assigned to rule over a family, over a village and over a clan. There were also chiefs who were given specific portfolios. All adult daughters automatically came under this category of chiefs. Their specific portfolio or duty, as chiefs, was to act as secret agents for their fathers' lineage. So, as soon as a daughter was born, she received the title, 'Chief', and an assignment as secret agent to be assumed when she became an adult.

Since daughters were assigned this political title, chief, at birth, they were therefore political rulers in their own class. The title,

'Chief', went with them from their fathers' families to their marital homes. In other words, marriage did not change their status as Chief nor strip off their political duty assigned to them at birth. So, with this title, they had to continue performing related duty up into their marital homes.

Married daughters enjoyed the political power and accompanying duty for a long period of time. But there came a time when some of the married daughters had a second thought about the role they were playing for their father's lineage in times of inter-tribal land-related wars. Some of them did not care for their political status any more.

Now, married daughters were divided in opinion. Some loved the secret agent role and wanted to continue. Others did not think it was a good idea to continue performing this duty, especially where the wars resulted from land disputes between their father's and their husband's family or clan. They were no longer comfortable doing that because they themselves, their husbands and children suffered directly and indirectly the consequences of working as secret agents. So, they decided to stop doing that.

Two factions of married daughters now emerged -those who wanted to continue undercover work and those who did not like doing that anymore because of its negative impact on their marital families and withdrew. The struggle between the two factions lasted for a while. During that period, their combined efforts toward performing their assigned undercover agent duty were slowed down because of the distraction.

In the midst of this internal battle within the body of married daughters as a group, there came a certain season when many inter -village, inter-clan and inter-tribal land disputes were going on all at the same time. Some villages were involved in two or more land disputes. And some of the disputes led to regional wars.

Because too many wars were going on at the same time, the men thought daughters, married and unmarried, were not doing a good job in defending their clans or villages. So, the men planned to take over the rule and to appoint men to be secret agents.

By observation, the men came to know that some women were usually ill during the first three months of pregnancy. They also knew that many pregnant women usually had some difficulty moving themselves around in the last two months of pregnancy.

With this perception about pregnant women, the men struck. This is what they did: They impregnated all the daughters, married and unmarried, at the same time. "In that way, they will not be able to go to war anymore. Neither will they be able to comfortably travel to and fro working as secret agents during related wars," the men conspired against all the daughters.

The men succeeded. Their plan prevailed. Yes, during pregnancy period, the women could not perform this important duty, serving as secret agents, a duty that came with compensations. Also, before the men decided to take over, more than half of the married daughters had already stopped working as undercover agents for their fathers for reasons indicated above. As a group, daughters were now almost at zero point in terms of their political performance. Men then took over the role of secret agent and all accompanying political powers.

For all daughters, failure to perform their assigned duty effectively meant losing their political power as secret agent, status as ruler and title as chief. Married daughters were particularly and additionally affected as a result of the lapse in performing their duty. The six-feet land use injunction privilege formerly granted to them by their fathers was no longer guaranteed. So, married daughters did not only lose the title, chief. They lost the guaranteed six-feet land space compensation as well.

However, the continued practice of the custom - taking a married daughter back at death to her family to be buried near her fathers or ancestors, shows that women did not lose the land space compensation in its entirety. The tradition has survived, even though it has been relaxed. In recent times, when a married woman dies, there is more flexibility regarding where she should be buried. The final decision usually depends on whether her family can afford the burial cost or wants to do it.

Nowadays, the woman's family (extended family male member, father or brother) or the husband's family (husband, her son(s) or if the husband is deceased, the immediate oldest male member in the husband's family) has the prerogative to decide where the woman should be laid to rest. In an unusual circumstance, even the son-in-law may contest for the corpse of his beloved mother-in-law.

If the woman was a widow and was a good wife who was also kind to everybody in the extended family, the step-sons want to show her that they do love her even though she had no son of her own. If she was a good sister, her brothers want her to know that they had not forgotten her kindness and the love she had for them when she was alive.

If the deceased widow had a grown-up son, the son wants to pay the last respect to his mother for the sacrifices she made for him to have a good life. He may choose to bury the mother near to or by the side of her husband /his father if the husband had already gone, or where the husband chose before he passed.

The son-in-law had vowed to give his mother-in-law a descent burial, even though she had no son of her own. He is now ready to fight with intensity over the corpse to keep the promise he made to his wife's mother when she was alive, and to show her that he still loves her up to the end of her life on Earth. One way to express that love and to keep that promise is to give her the 6-feet land space on his property.

Not long ago, an incident was reported in my father's extended family where the body of a deceased widow with a married daughter, who was also the only child to the mother, was almost torn apart as a result of problems between the woman's step-sons and her son-in-law over where she should be laid to rest.

In some situations, there could be a serious verbal or/and physical fights among son-in-law, the woman's relatives from her father's side and her husband's family over where she should be. Such show is common where the woman was a widow and had no grown up son of her own, or where the married daughter is the woman's only child.

Anyway, since the time all the daughters lapsed in performing this very important duty - spying for their fathers' lineage in times of land-related wars, the custom of a daughter automatically becoming a ruler and a chief in any capacity from birth in her father's family up into her husband's home was not even made optional. The practice was abrogated. It totally ended.

For a long time, women did not get back their ruling power until not too long ago. Nowadays, women all over the world are gradually reclaiming their political or ruling powers. Many have held prominent positions in politics. Some have become high ranking rulers in their countries, and have received chieftaincy and even higher titles in their respective villages, countries as well as in inter-national agencies.

THE WHIRLDWIND THAT CAME TO HELP HUMANS IN FARM WORK

In Nigerian-Ibibio culture, a deity called, *Idio*, was once believed to control farming and farm yields. Its origin is traced back to when a whirlwind swept furiously across newly-burnt farmlands and cleared them (*atang otok*) in a twinkle of an eye.

When the farmers saw the work of the wind, they were astonished. It so happened that the whirlwind concentrated only on the largest farm lands cleared for cultivation that year. To the people, this incident was the most unexplainable part of the event. "This is a miracle. Maybe, the god wants farm yields from the largest plots to be used in offering sacrifice to him," they pondered. Soon, they believed without any doubt that the wind was indeed a god who came down to help them in farm work.

To bring this god nearer home so that it would continue to increase crop yields and protect harvest, each farmer decided to build a shrine for it in his yam barn in his yard and offered sacrifices yearly to the god.

Since the whirlwind swept through the largest farm land in every family, the farmers in each family unanimously decided, after the miraculous incident, to designate the largest of the farm plots in each family as Idio plot (*Ikot Idio*). This plot was held in trust by the oldest living male elder in the family. And it was taken over by the next oldest living male only after the death of the former. This land or plot could not be sold for any reason.

I tend to assume that before the idio incident, the concept of leaving the largest family farmland in the trust of the most senior of the elders in every family was already in practice. And since this elder was the one who usually conducted regular sacrifices to the family god or gods, anyway, performing idio rituals naturally came under his duties as the religious head in the family.

The origin of *Idio* is legendary -an event regarded as historical and believed to have taken place, although it may or may not have happened. However, the relics of idio land holding practice in today's Ibibio culture make the related event believable, although not verifiable. For our fore-fathers, ancestors, Idio concept was real. They practiced it and observed the custom, and worshiped the related god and believed in its efficacy in bringing about good yearly harvest.

Many families have continued to observe this custom, although in part. It seems the land holding aspect is mostly emphasized in practice in modern times. Of course, we should not overlook the economic benefit for the trustee. But the ritualistic worship of the god and the belief in its power to bring about good yearly farm yields seem to be fading away, or are practiced in a few communities.

In some parts of Nigeria-Ibibio, *idio* plot is called *ikot okpon editem*, which means "a plot

farmed by the oldest elder in the family."
This phrase simply describes which elder in
the family is supposed to farm this plot and
under whose trust the land should remain.

I grew up to see idio concept put to
practice in my father's extended family. For
the first time in my life, I heard the term, *ikot
okpon editem,* from my father's only brother
in 1967. Right after my father passed in auto
accident in April of that year, his brother
came to me and started talking about the
rights tradition had granted him to claim the
largest among all the farm plots my father
had, a plot that was under my father's control
and trust when he was alive.

"A plot that my mother usually cultivated,
and I and my siblings helped in planting
cassava and other crops? No, that can not be!"
I was determined and ready to fight to the
end. "Why does he want to take this particular piece of land, in addition to his own
share of inherited pieces of farm-land?"
ignorantly, I did challenge my uncle.

Maybe my uncle attempted to explain why

he, now being the oldest elder in his father's family, had to take over that piece of land and hold it in his trust. But I got my mind made up, "He can not take my father's share of farm plot while I am still breathing."

Until one of my father's friends came and explained the custom to me, I refused to know, acknowledge or understand this idio land holding practice. Even after many years, I still did not get it until during the course of researching for my work on naming practices and other related works a few years ago. Now I know that the term, *ikot okpon editem* and *Ikot Idio* refer to one and the same thing.

[*You see*! Ignorance can cause one to fight blindly. Now that I have come to understand what my uncle was trying to tell me, I feel extremely embarrassed and ashamed for challenging him blindly. I really feel bad now that I look back. He has forgiven me, I guess.

That is not all. I am sure I insulted my uncle in the process of questioning the *idio* tradition he attempted to preserve. *At this point, I do apologize to whomever, living or dead, I offended in the course of ignorance-ridden, blind fight I embarked on to defend and preserve my father's estate at all cost*]

As a genuine and committed defender of good traditions, I am therefore obliged to offer a word of advice to the present and future generations: It is an unavoidable *commission* for all of us to learn and know our traditions, present and past, bad and good, what used to be and what has survived. In that way, we will not be ignorant of what to fight for, when to fight, and when not to fight and let it be, especially if the custom is not harmful or does not hurt anyone in any way, economically, emotionally, physically or spiritually.

Fighting for something *blindly* is not only embarrassing, especially when we later find out that we were really wrong, and we truly insulted our elders in the process. It also exposes our *ignorance*. We then have to gain a reasonable amount of knowledge about some things we care about, particularly those traditions we consider worth knowing and fighting for to preserve. An awareness of what is and what used to be culturally is likely to help us clearly discern what to fight for and what not to, especially when we are confronted by well-informed or knowledgeable elders who are also genuine defenders and keepers of traditions.

Moreover, we can give only what we have. And we can share with others only what we know or have custody of. If we have to tell others about our tradition, the information about a given custom must be correct. If an elder wants to pass down an ancient tradition by words of mouth or in writing to the young generation, the information about that particular custom must be correct.

It is important to note that not all elders are knowledgeable in these things, I mean their cultural traditions. Many have partial knowledge about them partly because of their lack of interest. Some learned by listening to elders in the family describe their traditions in casual conversations. Some elders learned through participating in related rituals or by being a member of a family where such rituals were practiced. Others witnessed others in the community participate in or perform related rituals.

Also, there are those who were not privileged to be born into families where pertinent customs were practiced. In some families, one to three generations of their members were born into a foreign culture. As a result, grand-parents and parents may not know pertinent traditional practices of their indigenous culture. So they can not impart to their children or grandchildren or pass down what they themselves do not know nor understand.

Many parents and grandparents born outside their native culture have not had the opportunity to see related customs in practice nor heard about them from anyone. But if anyone of them is interested and is genuinely determined to understand her or his culture so as to live it meaningfully, the person can learn any cultural aspect of his or her choice through self-directed studies. These may include reading relevant books or/and talking to individuals who are knowledgeable in relevant areas.

These may be the right and easy ways to learn the native culture because either of the methods is relatively less threatening than other routes. Reading relevant books, or/and asking the right questions at the right places and getting answers from those who know are other ways to learn, especially for those who do not have the opportunity to learn in a formal classroom.

Parents and community or family elders therefore have to joyfully assume their responsibility, a necessary burden to learn their traditions so as to pass them down to their children with enough clarity and accuracy.

By the way, the word, idio, is used in this context as a verb, and it means, "Come." Here, someone is calling everybody from a distance to come and see what he or she has seen. If I say, "Idi-o," I am calling people to come and see or witness with me the strange and unusual sight I have seen. In Nigerian-

Ibibio English, the word, Idio-o, would therefore be "Come-o."

"Idio" seems to be what the farmer who was the first to see the miraculous work of the whirlwind said or did. In extreme awe, wonder or excitement, he called out in a loud voice, inviting other people to come and see what he saw. In the process of trying to figure out and assign a name to the whirlwind wonder, the people attached the word idio to the land holding practice that originated from that incident.

In modern times, the word has taken up additional metaphors. Idio is also identified with extraordinary hard work or high-level energy to work faster than others, in farm work or in any other project one sets out to accomplish. Anyone who works extra fast or hard on a project could be described as idio.

In addition, since the whirlwind incident, some parents have had the option to name their child, Idio, if the child is born in the year in which the parents cultivate this plot. Naming a child after this god may not necessarily be a bad decision in the sense that the god in itself may not be harmful. But even where the rituals to acknowledge the related god's power are no longer necessary, the mere fact that a child is named after this deity invites soul-tie related problems or negative entanglement into the life of the child.

In his discussion on demonology and deliverance, David Okumgba defines soul-tie as "the spiritual knitting of the souls of two persons to the magnitude that it allows the spirit operating in one person to gain access to the life of the other." In the context of this work, it is the knitting of the soul of the child and that of the god, if the god has a soul.

Soul-tie could be positive or negative. It could negatively create unhealthy elements of control and manipulation indirectly or consciously, especially where the child, now an adult, does not recognize its power through regular sacrifice where or if necessary.

Based on the possible entanglement with negative soul-tie elements, parents are *not* encouraged to give their children names of local gods. Even where the parents think the said god did or does something good for them, that excuse is not worth starting their children on a wrong foot as soon as they land on Earth. Many who give their children such names are not even aware of the damage they have done to their babies who just join the world family.

Sometimes, parents argue that the soul-tie with the god in question is positive. Whether the tie is positive or negative, the mere fact that a child's life is entangled with a local deity may set the child up for failure in life. Positive or negative link does not remove the consequences of soul-tie. Even where they think that after all, the regular sacrifice to the god is no more involved, the negative impact could still be there. All parents need to be aware of this.

I am not quite sure of how much of idio ritual is practiced in modern times. But I want to emphasize this: Naming a child after a god could be detrimental to a child's life in general, his/her identity and/or destiny in particular. By doing this, parents unknowingly establish a negative soul-tie between the child and the deity. The best gifts from us parents to our children, as a way of welcoming our children into the world family, are destiny enhancing names that provide them with a fresh, clean start in life.

Giving our children the *right* names is a responsibility every parent must undertake with joy and with full spiritual awareness of what they are doing for and to their children. We should therefore avoid giving our children names with negative meanings, names with repulsive or obnoxious connotations or negatively engulfing names.

Every parent needs to also know that a good name is not necessarily the right name for the child. In this discourse, a good name is a name with positive meaning. A bad name has a negative meaning. But a right name is a name that enhances destiny achievement or that is in alignment with the divine plan for our lives on Earth. Anyone who is interested in the topic that deals with the impact of personal names on the bearers may read this author's work on culture of names.

HOW WOMEN CAME TO WEAR
TWO WRAPPERS AT A TIME

There lived a couple, a husband and a wife. They were not very rich and they were planning to do something to improve their lives financially. But something tragic suddenly happened. The husband went to bed one night and never woke up again. He passed on while sleeping.

The wife wept and wept and would not receive any comfort. But she had friends who were there for her during this tragic moment. They helped her to recover emotionally from the loss. She gradually recovered. Even with that, she missed her husband badly.

The woman was now a widow, a very poor widow. I mean poor. She was poorer than when the husband was alive. When he was alive, each one of them had a small piece of wrapper to wear in the house. They also had only one larger piece of wrapper that both of them shared for wearing outside or going out.

The couple never went out together at the same time to any place because they had only this one wrapper for use outside the house. So, if the husband wanted to go out on a given day at a given time to take care of some business, he would use the wrapper to go out. And the wife would have to wait for the husband to return home. After the husband got back home, the wife would then take that same wrapper from the husband and wear it to probably the same place the husband went to, to the market, farm or to attend any other engagements.

After the husband passed, she continued to use that wrapper. Now, she was the only one to use it. At home, she also used the small piece that belonged to her husband and her own. But there came a time when the small wrappers she usually wore at home were all torn. Soon, the widow was left with only the one she usually wore when going out.

As time went on, the widow was so poor that she had only one piece of wrapper for use both at home and when going out. She had no other clothes, such as head-ties, brassieres, blouses nor under-pants. All what she had to cover her body was one piece of wrapper. [Today, the normal length of a wrapper is usually a two-yard fabric] And she wore that one wrapper to everywhere, to the farm, to the market, to the stream to fetch water and to the woods to get firewood.

At home, the widow went naked because she did not want the wrapper to get dirty too soon. If a visitor knocked at her door, she would quickly put on the wrapper before she opened the door. On cold nights, she would also use it to cover herself.

Sometimes, the woman accidentally dropped some crumbs of food on the wrapper when eating. She had sat on dirty chairs many times. Sometimes there were sticky food crumbs on those chairs, and the crumbs would stick to the back of her wrapper, and it was usually around the buttocks area. Whenever that happened, she would not wash the stained spots immediately. For months, she would wear the wrapper without washing it.

Occasionally, water touched that wrapper when it rained, and only if the rain met the woman outside wearing it to or from somewhere. If the wrapper was really dirty, she would wash it at night. Of course, she would dare not wash it on cold nights because she would have nothing to cover herself and keep warm.

The widow was a farmer and usually sweated badly when she worked on the farm. So, if the wrapper stunk badly because of sweat, she would also wash it at night. But she did not wash it quite often. Maybe, she did it once in three months.

At some point, the wrapper began to smell because the woman was not washing off the spots stained by food crumbs right after it was soiled. And that smell attracted fat house rats. The rats began to eat up the spots on the wrapper covered with smelly sticky food drops. This is what got her. Gradually, the wrapper wore out. There were holes, big and small, in front, at the back, on the sides and all over it. The biggest holes were at the back, right around her buttocks area.

The woman was usually embarrassed whenever she went somewhere wearing this wrapper with holes. "This is no good any more," the widow lamented. "What am I going to do now?" she became greatly worried. She then began to think harder about what she should do next now that her only wrapper was no longer covering her nakedness.

In those days, there were no needles nor threat. Neither were there any sewing machines with which she could have sewn or mended the wrapper. So, she could not close up the holes by using thread and needle to sew by hand or by using the sewing machine.

Quickly, the widow recalled, "Oh! My husband left behind a piece of land for me to farm." That was the only farmland the family had. And that was also the only inheritance from her husband. She thought of selling it and using the money to buy a new wrapper for herself. "But how can I sell it? If I sell the only farmland I have, where will I plant crops?" she had a second thought.

"Yes, I can sell this land and use the money to buy wrapper," the widow almost convinced herself. "But what will I eat if I have no land to plant vegetables and yams, and sell some to buy other things I need?" she pondered.

"I have a better idea," the widow figured out another way to tackle the problem. That idea was to sell half of the farm plot, instead of selling the whole piece of plot. She finally convinced herself that selling half of the farm plot was the best thing to do, the best of the best. That was exactly what she did. She sold part of the land. And that gave her more than enough money to buy a new piece of wrapper. She used the remaining part of the money to start a small business, selling wrappers.

After the widow had bought a new 2-yard piece of wrapper, she did not throw away the old one with holes. She started to use that at home instead of going naked as she did in the past. Sometimes, she would also wear the old ragged wrapper under first, and then wear the new one over it. When wearing the two wrappers, she usually arranged them in a certain way. She would tie the old torn one from the waist, and let it drape down to her ankles. She would then wear the new one from above the breast and let it drape down to below the knee and a little above the ankles.

Once again, the widow was able to cover her nakedness, and that, lavishly. And she felt good about herself. That was not all. By doing this, she invented, without realizing what she did, a new style or way of using the wrapper in the process. This new or emerging fashion or style is what has come to be known in recent times as *ndot iba*, an outfit where two wrappers are worn at a time, one on top of the other, and neither of the two wrappers has to be torn one.

Ndot iba has become a stable fashion style since then. In today's Nigeria, it can be worn with a blouse made of the same fabric as that of the wrapper or some other matching color of fabric. This fashion is no longer a poor widow's fashion style. It has permanently remained a preferred style for every respecttable Nigerian woman, especially in the southeastern part of the country. And the fashion is suitable for all occasions. One can dress up or down, depending on accessories and occasions. I have many pairs of ndot iba, some with blouses of the same fabrics as those of the wrappers. And I love them all.

Later, the widow designed another brand new fashion wear out of the old torn wrapper. She was not even aware of what she did in terms of adding to the existing fashions. When she initially started to wear the old torn wrapper under the new one, she usually turned the parts with real big holes to the sides. As time went on, she created something else out of it.

One day, she laid the old wrapper with

holes on the floor, put a rope across it length-wise, and folded it into two. She wore the stringed wrapper, now shorter, on her waist and adjusted it to fit her waist. Before she knew it, she already made a short skirt out of it. She then began to wear it as an under-skirt and wore her new wrapper over it.

Of course, the woman later became more creative than before in using the wrapper and the stringed shorter wrapper. She had the choice to wear the shorter under-wrapper when using one or two wrappers at a time. And her choice depended on the type of social context, occasion or the wearer's readiness to dress up or down. At home, she would wear the short under-wrapper with or without the bigger wrapper over it, nor a blouse with it. And her preference was also dictated by the household environment or the weather.

This short wrapper with a string used as underwear at the time is what later became known as *mkpin*. Mkpin is very similar to the short under-wear women wear nowadays. But in those days, it was initially used as we wear the Western style of under-pants or brief called, *iba efud,* nowadays in Ibibio language. If it was worn with a dress, a full body size underwear (*ofong adaha idem*) without or with straps on the shoulders was worn over the mkpin, and then the dress over the underwear.

Mkpin was always worn far down from below the belly button, just as we wear briefs in recent times. But the length of a typical mkpin was usually up to the knee. A longer mkpin was sometimes designed, specifically to be worn mainly at home with or without a blouse, a dress nor a wrapper over it. It was particularly preferred during hot weather.

Of course, if the length of mkpin is beyond the knee, the wearer may be 'dragging' it." On page 29 of his *Mutanda Oyom Namondo,* Nkanga uses the metaphor, "*ekpot nte mkpin*" which means, "They dragged like mkpin," to describe how tired and exhausted the people were after dancing *Ekombi* throughout the night. He likens how sluggishly they dragged themselves along to go home after a busy night of dancing to how the longer, bogus style of mkpin drags down behind the wearer.

I grew up to see my mother's aunty wear mkpin. I even saw my mother using it for a brief period of time. Later, she completely switched to Western style under-pants. In recent times, mkpin has been replaced by underpants called, iba efud, in Nigerian-Ibibio language.

Remember: It was a poor widow who accidentally and later by necessity invented the use of two wrappers at a time as a fashion style as well as the use of *mkpin*.

WHEN ALMIGHTY GOD WITHDREW FROM THE EARTH

The Almighty God, who now lives in the sky, originally lived with humans on Earth long ago. During the period God was on Earth, He created everything: humans, trees, animals, fire, water, and heat, light and all other living and non-living things. He made sure that everything he created functioned properly.

After creating these things, God assigned His servants to control everything else, except the Sun. He supervised them to make sure all what He created worked well. God did not assign His servants to control the Sun because He had a special interest in the Sun. He, instead, directly controlled the Sun, light, fire and heat because they were all located in

His compound. He decided to take up this responsibility himself for safety reasons.

It was Sun that gave light, fire and heat. Since Sun was in God's compound, people had to walk down there everyday to get fire. Some used dry leaves to get the fire. Some used dry wood. Others used firebrand (*emuum ikang* - a small bundle of dry wine palm tree stem cut into pieces like chewing or chop sticks specifically designed for this purpose. The charcoal and ashes from the dry wooden fire brands made God's compound dirty. And the people did not make any effort to remove the litters or clean up behind themselves.

When God observed how humans were using Sun, He saw that some of them were very careless in handling their firebrands. They were careless to a point where they sometimes dropped burning fire brands at places they should not. So, God was afraid that if He was not careful, someday humans could burn down His house or burn Him to death as a result of their carelessness. To avoid his house and Him being burnt down,

God was then determined to be very vigilant over how the people used the Sun.

For some people, God's compound was too far from where they lived. So, they had to walk some distance everyday to God's compound to get fire. Soon, those who lived farther away from God's compound began to complain that their feet were hurting because of walking a long distance everyday to get fire. They also complained that they did not have enough heat and light because the Sun was too far away from where they lived.

The people even questioned and blamed God for keeping the fire in His compound and having a full control over it. "Those who live near you get more fire, more light and more heat than we do," those who lived farther away accused God of being partial. "You are not fair to everybody," they also said God favored those who lived near Him.

God, in response to their complaints, told the people that he was not partial at all. Rather, He was trying to be careful so that His house would not be burnt down. He also explained to them how careless some of them were in using their firebrands. "Okay! "I'm moving the Sun to the center of the world and I am not going to control it anymore." God decided. And He did as He said.

When the heat of the Sun became unbearable, too hot for anybody to bear, the people went back to God and complained about the excessive heat. "Probably He wants all of us dead," the people thought. At some point, they even concluded that God and his servants were out to kill all of them, W*ap*, at a time.

God laughed at them and said, "How can I destroy what I made?" He then took the Sun back to His compound. As soon as God did that, the people started again to go to God's compound to get fire. What God feared most eventually happened to Him. The people became even more careless than before. They made God's compound dirtier than ever. And the worst was yet to come.

When God took the Sun back to His compound, some people became so angry that they burned down parts of God's compound. That was not all. Almost half of God's house was burnt down as a result of the people's carelessness in using firebrand. The worst was when some half-burnt fire brands the people dropped carelessly also burned God's feet. This was what pissed God's servants off the most, "Burned God's feet!"

At this point, God's servants were very angry with those who were careless in using their fire-brands and those who were angry with God for taking the Sun back to His yard. "Enough! That's it! No more!" they yelled at the people, urging them to stop burning God's feet and house. Tired of the people's reckless behaviors, God's servants quickly went to God and suggested, "Why not take away the Sun from the Earth and be through with it."

God was not happy to see His compound so dirty. Neither did He plan to take the Sun away from the Earth. He thought He could manage and tolerate that particular human behavior - recklessness. But when the people also burned His feet and parts of His house,

He could no longer bear such behaviors by humans.

Being very angry with the people, God said, "Enough is enough. I don't think I can ever satisfy these people." God told His servants how frustrated He was in dealing with the men and women He created, "No matter how hard I try to please them, they still complain and complain, mumble and grumble."

At this point, God was tired of being tossed around by humans. He realized that He could not satisfy them in any way or form. He was no longer ready to continue to put up with the terrible behaviors they exhibited. God then decided, "I can not live with them on Earth anymore." So, He took off with his servants and carried Sun along with Him to the sky. Since then till today, God and the Sun have lived together happily in the sky.

MOTHER THUNDER AND
HER SON, LIGHTENING

Once upon a time, Thunder and Lightening lived among people on Earth. Thunder was the mother of Lightening, and she had a very bad temper. She was not angry often. But whenever she was angry, she would release stony bullets which usually killed those living around their house. She would burn houses and farms. She would knock down trees and destroy anything that was on her way.

Learning from his mother, Lightening also caused harm to their neighbors whenever he was angry. His temper was not as terrible as his mother's. But he sometimes struck people on their eyes and caused them to become blind. When he struck, people and animals would be very scared. Sometimes, the fowls would scream and run for their lives to a nearby shelter. As Lightening grew up, his temper got worse than that of his mother.

There came a time when the neighbors and people who lived in the same city with them could no longer bear the noise and the damage Thunder and Lightening usually caused to the people, animals, plants and other things. So, members in their community and nearby cities reported the mother and the son to the king of their city.

The king called Thunder and her son and warned them to stop causing damage to people's farms and lives. But they did not stop roaring, striking and destroying lives and property in the process. When the people continued to complain about their lousy and destructive behaviors, the king ordered Thunder and Lightening to leave the Earth.

Thunder and Lightening left the Earth and moved to the sea. In the sea, they also showed their anger. Thunder would release her booming voice and that usually disturbed the fish and all other animals in the sea.

Even land animals that lived around the sea were also disturbed. And they also grumbled about Thunder's and her son's loud noises. Lightening would come to the surface of the water and strike whenever he was angry.

All the animals in the water were usually scared to death because of the strange noise they started to hear lately. The disturbance was so much that all the animals in and around the sea told them to leave their kingdom because they were too noisy to be anyone's neighbor.

Thunder and her son, Lightening, could not return to Earth because they were kicked out of it earlier as a result of their destructive behaviors. The only option they had was to go to the sky. "If we are kicked out of the sky, where else will we go?" Thunder and her son thought of moving to the sky. So that they would not be thrown out of the sky, she and her son planned to behave differently when they got there. "We must cut off all the noises and stop damaging people's lives and things," they warned themselves.

When they got to the sky, Lightening did not stop striking. So, his mother warned him, telling him to stop striking so that they would not be driven out of the sky. "If that happens, we will have no other place to move to," she reminded her son. So, Thunder was determined to keep Lightening in check.

While there in the sky, Thunder would call out in a loud voice whenever her son started striking, "Stop! Stop! Stop!" The mother would yell at him until he stopped. Sometimes, the son listened and stopped right away. At other times, he would stubbornly continue to strike. Sometimes, the mother would be so tired and frustrated that she would have no more energy or strength to scream telling him to stop. Even after the mother had stopped rebuking him, he would not care but continue to do his thing, anyway.

So, whenever we hear the thunder roaring, we should know that she is warning her son, lightening, to cut off his anger and stop striking. If thunder continues to roar after the lightening had stopped, she is simply reminding him not to dare strike again so that they are not thrown out of the sky. If lightening continues, it means thunder is either tired of telling him to stop, is sleeping or is sick, lying in bed and not able to speak. If he continues, maybe he is angry over something or is hungry and wants to eat badly.

Luckily, soon after they arrived in the sky Thunder and her son discovered that there were no human beings or animals living in the sky. That meant they had no neighbors, and as such, no-one complained about their noises. So, they decided to spend the rest of their lives in the sky. This may be why thunder and lightening are now living in the sky and doing their own thing.

WHEN THE SUN MOVED
TO THE SKY

Many, many years ago, Sun and Sea lived together on Earth. They were great friends. Sun was very fond of Sea. So was Sea of Sun. Their friendship went on for many years. During those years, Sun visited Sea quite often. But Sea never went to Sun's house.

One day, Sun thought, "Wait a minute! Why has Sea not visited me ever since we have been friends?" Sun decided to go and talk to Sea about the matter during his next visit.

"We have been friends for many years. But you have never one day come to my house. Why is it so?" Sun asked Sea. Sea's reply was that Sun's house was too small for her. "If I dare to come to your house, you will have to run away and leave the whole house for me," Sea explained to Sun what would happen if she visited him. Sun promised to move to a larger house if Sea really wanted to visit him.

Sea agreed to go to Sun's house for dinner on the next day. Sun was very happy to hear that Sea had agreed to visit him. Sun told Sea that she would be free to occupy all the rooms in his house, except one room. He bargained with Sea to leave just one room for him. "There has to be a dry room for us to enjoy our dinner," Sun explained to Sea.

In reply, Sea said to Sun, "I always live and do all my things in wet places; but for your sake, I'll try to control myself." Sea told Sun that she was not quite sure whether she would be able to control herself when she got to Sun's house. Sun promised to help Sea function or do things for the first time in her life in a dry place.

Sun's new house had eight rooms. Sun prepared dinner and set it in one room. The room was beautifully decorated with rose flowers. Spoons, forks and plates were made of silver and gold. Napkins were of assorted colors and shapes, and were made of the most beautiful and expensive linen in the world.

Now, Sea was at Sun's house. By the doorsteps she stood. She then knocked at the door. With all excitement, Sun opened the door and welcomed Sea into his house. When Sea went into the sitting room, Sun reached out his hand to shake her hand. But Sea did not stretch out her hand to shake Sun's hand. Neither did she sit down when Sun offered her a seat in the sitting room. Before Sun knew what was going on, Sea had already rushed in and covered the whole sitting room with water.

"Control yourself! Control your-self!" Sun yelled at Sea asking her to stop. Was Sea able to control herself? No.

Immediately, Sun ran into one of the rooms. Sea followed him and covered that room with water. Wherever in the house Sun ran to, Sea followed. "Let me go into the room set for dinner," Sun thought if he went in there and locked the door, Sea would not dare to pursue him into that room. As soon as Sun opened the door to get into that special room, Sea also rushed in and filled up the room with water. Even after the door was locked, that did not stop Sea getting in there.

"Stop! Stop! You need to control yourself," Sun told Sea in a very loud voice. But Sea could not. Running for his life, Sun jumped out and sat on the roof top of his house. While on the roof top, Sun started to plead with Sea, "Can you just leave my house and go back to your house, please!"

By this time, Sun was very upset because the whole house was flooded. Worst of all, the dinner he spent a lot of money on and time to prepare for two of them was floating on the water. The silver dinner plates had sunk to the bottom of the water, down on the floor. The gold and silver spoons, knives and forks were no where to be seen. They all sank to the bottom, the floor under the water. The napkins were floating on the water.

Sea could not control herself as she said she would try to. Neither could Sun help Sea control herself as he promised. When Sun saw that Sea had covered his house from bottom to the top of the roof and his entire compound, Sun ran to the sky to save his life. Since that incident, Sun and Sea were no more friends. And they never lived together again on Earth. This is why Sun and Sea now live separately.

A Nigerian-Ibibio proverb traced to this incident goes like this in the native language: *Utin utin aka nnung inyang? Inyang isikaa nnung utin?* In English it is: Is it only the sun that goes to the sea's house? Can the sea not visit the sun? What has now become a proverb is actually the question Sun asked himself as to why Sea never visited him. It was the question he asked before he decided to go and talk to Sea, and to suggest to her to find time and visit him.

We all have friends. Some live far away from us. As a result, we do not or can not visit them often, or never visited them at all. We only talk to them on the phone or write letters to them. We also have friends who live near to us. We may visit them once or many times in a week, in a month or in a year. If we visit our friends all the time, but they do not make any effort to visit us, we can ask ourselves the same question Sun asked himself. We can then use this proverb to tell them that it is time for them to visit or make plans to visit us.

CONCLUSION

Apart from increasing our knowledge base about some natural and super-natural phenomena and learning a few social skills, legends and myths are educative in some other ways. Reading or listening to legends, myths and other categories of folk tales can also enhance comprehension, and promote logical thinking and right guessing.

Also, reading about stories we learned during childhood years through word of mouth before we even went to school to learn reading definitely eases learning and makes learning enjoyable. And we learn better and with joy when we read about familiar events, concepts that affect our lives and issues we encounter daily in real life.

For many, some myths and legends may

appear to teach no moral values at all. Those of us who think this way may not be quite right. With a closer look, we will see that there is always something to learn from every story, at least one value to improve our quality of life in some way, in addition to its being just informative.

So, I strongly encourage parents, the elders and teachers in schools, both in formal and non-formal settings, to increase the current rate of teaching legends and myths to the same level or frequency we teach fables. In that way, we do not let our cultural traditions get lost during our generation. As we received these stories from our forefathers and foremothers, so should our children also have more or at least similar opportunities to receive same from us. This is an important obligation parents owe to their children.

ACKNOWLEDGEMENTS

I want to thank Bernadette Imeh, a friend I have not met in person but have talked with on the phone countless times, for her support and genuine friendship. Without her repeated explanations, the story on how women came to wear two wrappers at a time would not have been part of this discourse because I heard this story for the first time from her.

I also want to express my gratitude to Edet A. Udo who has retold the story in his book, *Who Are the Ibibio?* about how God withdrew from Earth and the origin of idio land holding practice. I also drew from his work on women as secret agents in times of land-related wars when I retold the tale on how women lost their ruling power.

The work of Elphinstone Dayrell, *Folk Stories from Southern Nigeria* drawn from a web forum, and that of E. N. Amaku, *Edikot Nwed Mbuk*, were also helpful in retelling the story on why the sun now lives in the sky. The Concise Encyclopedia was also a useful resource in defining the words, legend and myth.

About the Author

Emma Umana Clasberry is the author of many books - a continuation of her endeavor at African Peoples Institute (API) - a Chicago-based non-profit agency she founded with the purpose to promote cultural awareness and cultural pride among youth.

She has been a Subject of Biographical Record in *Who's Who of American Women*, 21st Edition, for Significant Contribution to the Betterment of Contemporary Society. Emma earned a B.A in Political Science and an M.A. in Urban Planning & Policy from University of Illinois at Chicago, and a Doctor of Education degree from California Coast University.

Emma focuses her interests in cultural studies as they relate to youth education and development, and how such knowledge can beef up cultural pride and positively impact economic welfare of young adults.

www.ingramcontent.com/pod-product-compliance
Lightning Source LLC
Chambersburg PA
CBHW060211290526
45789CB00003B/1239